ONE-PAGE   MARKETING   MASTERY:
SIMPLIFIED STRATEGIES FOR SUCCESS

Daniel D. Sims

CHAPTER 1

INTRODUCTION:EMBRACING SIMPLICITY IN MARKETING

Marketing might feel like a tangle of intricate techniques and creative concepts at times. In today's fast-paced world, however, embracing simplicity is a wise choice that may make your message stand out and connect with people deeply.

The Overload Era
Everywhere we turn, there is information - advertisements, social media, emails, you name it. It's simple for our minds to become overburdened. That is when simplicity comes into play. By keeping things

simple, you may assist your message to stand out and attract people's attention.

The Power of Simplicity

Consider simplicity to be a magic wand that changes your message into something strong and simple to grasp. Instead of including several facts, you select the most significant ones and deliver them in a clear and concise manner. This ensures that your message is understood without ambiguity.

Greetings, Clarity

Have you ever heard the phrase "less is more"? That is the essence of simplicity. When you simplify your marketing, you ensure that your message is clear. People immediately understand what you're presenting and why it's important to them. It's like turning on a light in a dark room; everything becomes more visible.

Making a Good First Impression

In a world when people's attention spans are limited, minimalism is your secret weapon. Consider that you just have a few seconds to make an impact. A simple message is like a supercharged arrow that instantly hits its target. People remember it since it is simple to understand.

Making Decisions Easier Complexity can lead to confusion, and confusion is bad for everyone. When you simplify your marketing, you help customers make faster judgments. They understand what you're presenting and can decide if it's what they're looking for without having to sift through layers of information

Trust is built via simplicity.
People choose things that are simple to grasp. When your marketing is straightforward, it appears honest and trustworthy. You are not concealing yourself behind sophisticated lingo or perplexing facts. You're being straightforward, which fosters trust between you and your audience.

Everyone Can Speak the Same Language
Simplicity is a language that everyone can understand, not just one group of people. A simple message can cross the gap regardless of where someone is from or what language they speak. It's a warm handshake that welcomes everyone to your brand.

The Long-Term Effect

When you embrace simplicity in your marketing, you create something that people remember. Simple messages are remembered because they are easy to remember. Your message becomes ingrained in their minds, and this is the kind of influence that can lead to long-term consumer connections.

In a Glimpse
Embracing simplicity in marketing is akin to amplifying your message. You're building a strong connection with your audience by keeping things simple, easy to comprehend, and relatable. In a world where attention is transitory, establishing your imprint and leaving a lasting impression requires simplicity.

CHAPTER 2

UNDERSTANDING YOUR AUDIENCE: KNOW YOUR IDEAL CUSTOMERS

One fundamental reality stands out in the wide world of marketing: the key to success is intimately knowing your audience. The crucial process of comprehending your ideal consumers is explored in this chapter, along with their wants, preferences, and habits. You may create effective marketing messages, establish deep connections, and eventually lead your company to success by analyzing the complex web of your audience.

The Science of Connection

A straightforward yet important principle—connecting with your audience on a human level—lays at the core of successful marketing. This connection is created by a thorough understanding of your prospective clients and what motivates them, not through generic messaging or broad generalizations. In short, marketing becomes a personalized experience that speaks directly to the needs and desires of your target demographic when you understand your audience instead of taking a one-size-fits-all strategy.

Beyond Demographics: Gaining Perspectives

Beyond simple demographics like age and gender, understanding your audience involves more. Investigating the specifics of their philosophies, drives, aspirations, and problems is important. With the help of this full picture of insights, you can predict your customers' actions, foresee their requirements, and present them with solutions that have a lasting emotional impact.

The Influence of Empathy

Understanding your audience requires empathy as its foundation. It involves putting yourself in your clients' shoes, seeing the world from their viewpoint, and experiencing their joys and difficulties. A connection that goes beyond transactional contacts and develops into genuine connections can be made when you learn to generate empathy for your audience.

The creation of buyer personas

The development of buyer personas is a potent strategy for gaining a knowledge of your audience. A detailed fictional representation of your ideal consumer is called a buyer persona. It contains details like demographics, tastes, actions, and problems. By developing these personas, you give your target market a face, enabling you to target your marketing initiatives with accuracy and empathy.

The Exploration Process

The process of learning about your audience is ongoing. It entails ongoing participation, research, and data analysis. It involves speaking with your customers, getting their opinions, and staying aware of how their requirements and tastes are changing. This dedication to comprehension guarantees that your marketing will continue to be timely, compelling, and efficient over time.

The Benefit of Digital

Understanding your audience has never been easier than it is in the modern digital world. Online tools, social networking sites, and analytics give a wealth of information that offers insights into the actions and interactions of your clients. Gaining a competitive edge by utilizing these digital tools enables you to fine-tune your marketing plans based on real-time feedback and trends.

Personalization: The Deepest Bond

Understanding your audience sets the door for personalisation, one of the most effective marketing techniques. A strong sense of connection and relevance is produced when you customize your messages, suggestions, and services for specific clients. Customers are more inclined to engage with, buy from, and promote your company if they feel heard and respected.

Rejecting presumptions

While it's crucial to comprehend your audience, it's also crucial to avoid forming assumptions. Making only assumptions can result in errors and lost opportunities. Instead, rely on data, research, and direct client interaction to inform your insights. This strategy makes sure that your knowledge is always current, correct, and in line with the needs of your target audience.

A Pathway to Impact

Understanding your audience requires constant effort and has a profound influence; it is not a static goal. Every element of your marketing strategy, from the messages you create to the distribution channels you pick, is influenced by it. Knowing your target clients very well gives you the ability to produce memorable experiences that resonate, connect, and motivate action.

CHAPTER 3

CRAFTING YOUR STRATEGY: BUILDING AN EFFECTIVE MARKETING PLAN

A well-crafted marketing strategy serves as a guiding beacon in the changing and competitive landscape of modern company, illuminating the route to success. "Crafting Your Strategy: Building an Effective Marketing Plan," Chapter 3, looks into the critical process of developing a comprehensive and strategic marketing plan. Businesses can negotiate the intricacies of the market with clarity and purpose by meticulously establishing goals, selecting ideal techniques, and aligning activities with the larger vision.

The Roadmap to Success

A marketing strategy is analogous to a building blueprint. It offers an organized framework outlining the stages, resources, and techniques required to attain specified goals. A well-crafted marketing plan sketches out the road toward reaching and resonating with the target audience, just like an architect anticipates the finished project before constructing the foundation.

Setting Specific Goals

A set of clear and quantifiable goals is at the foundation of a good marketing plan. These goals function as beacons that direct all marketing efforts. Whether the goal is to raise brand awareness, improve sales, or launch a new product, well-defined objectives create a feeling of purpose and direction, ensuring that every activity is aligned with the anticipated outcomes.

Navigating the five Ws and one H

In order to create a marketing plan, you must first answer the following questions: Who, What, When, Where, Why, and How. Who is the intended audience? What are the main messages and products? When will the campaign be launched? Where will it be carried out? What difference does it make? How will it be put in place and measured? Precision in answering these questions creates the framework for a thorough and unified marketing approach.

Segmenting and focusing

Segmentation is a vital component of developing a successful marketing strategy. The target audience is divided into separate groups based on shared criteria like demographics, behaviors, and preferences. Businesses can adjust their messaging and techniques to each section once they've identified them, increasing the relevancy and impact of their marketing efforts.

Choosing Effective Tactics

A systematic selection of strategies that correspond with the goals and preferences of the target audience is required for an effective marketing plan. These strategies can include social media campaigns, content production, email marketing, influencer collaborations, and other activities. The objective is to select strategies that not only resonate with the audience but also capitalize on the brand's strengths.

The Integrated Strategy

Marketing efforts in the digital age are no longer limited to a single medium. An integrated approach that leverages numerous platforms and channels, on the other hand, ensures maximum reach and impact. A comprehensive and harmonious integration of strategies improves the overall success of the marketing campaign by providing customers with a consistent experience across multiple touchpoints.

Budget Management and Resource Allocation

An efficient marketing strategy includes wise budgeting and resource management. It is critical to identify the financial resources available for the marketing campaign and effectively distribute them to different techniques. Furthermore, resource allocation encompasses aspects other than money, such as human resources, time, and technology.

Develop Key Performance Indicators (KPIs)

Measurable outcomes are critical to the success of a marketing strategy. Key Performance Indicators (KPIs) serve as benchmarks for assessing the campaign's efficacy. KPIs give a quantitative framework for analyzing success and making data-driven adjustments, whether it's tracking website traffic, conversion rates, social media engagement, or sales figures.

Adaptability and flexibility

While a marketing plan provides a planned blueprint, maintaining a degree of flexibility and adaptation is critical. The corporate environment is fluid, and unexpected difficulties or opportunities may occur. A strong marketing strategy is one that can pivot and modify strategies in real time in response to changing market conditions.

Partnership and communication

Collaboration and open communication among diverse stakeholders are required for a well-crafted marketing plan. To guarantee that the plan is carried out smoothly, marketing teams, creative departments, sales teams, and leadership must all work together. Effective communication channels generate a sense of unity and purpose by facilitating the flow of ideas, feedback, and insights.

The Leadership Role

Leadership is essential in developing and carrying out a marketing strategy. Effective leadership, whether provided by a startup founder, a business owner, or a marketing executive, offers the vision, advice, and support required to match the marketing strategy with the overall business objectives. In reaction to changing market
circumstances, leadership sets the tone for flexibility and innovation.

CHAPTER 4

CREATING COMPELLING CONTENT: ENGAGING MESSAGES THAT RESONATE

Content is king in the world of modern marketing. "Creating Compelling Content: Engaging Messages that Resonate," Chapter 4, looks into the art and science of generating messages that fascinate, inspire, and establish long-term connections with the audience. Businesses may use the power of storytelling to leave an everlasting mark on their target audience by knowing the aspects that lead to great content and mastering the strategies that generate engagement.

The Connection's Pulse

The lifeblood of effective communication is compelling content. It's the link that links businesses on a deeper level with their target audience. Businesses may convey their beliefs, offers, and stories in an emotionally and intellectually captivating way through intriguing content. It is the art of creating communications that go beyond information to elicit emotions, ignite dialogues, and develop relationships.

The Components of Engaging Content

A compelling piece of content consists of several important aspects that work together to catch and maintain attention. These components are as follows:

Authenticity: The foundation of compelling material is authenticity. It reflects the brand's own voice and values, establishing trust and relatability with the audience. Genuine content has the ability to humanize a brand, making it more approachable and likable.

Relevance: Content that speaks directly to the audience's needs, goals, and concerns is intrinsically captivating. When material connects with the audience's experiences, an immediate connection is formed, which drives additional engagement.

Storytelling: Storytelling is at the heart of all compelling content. Humans are hardwired to respond to tales, and well-crafted stories may take the audience to another realm. Storytelling gives content depth, emotion, and relatability, making it memorable and effective.

Content that is visually beautiful is compelling. It uses high-quality photographs, graphics, videos, and design components to improve the entire user experience. Visual aesthetics are critical in grabbing attention and efficiently transmitting information.

Value

Engaging material provides value to the audience. It gives readers or viewers insights, knowledge, entertainment, or solutions that improve their lives. Content that provides immediate gratification is more likely to be shared and remembered.

The Influence of Emotion

Emotion is the secret ingredient that transforms ordinary content into engaging content. The audience responds to emotionally resonant information with laughter, empathy, inspiration, or nostalgia. People develop a deeper connection with a company when they feel something while engaging with information, making them more inclined to remember and share the message.

Message Tailoring to the Audience

Audiences are the focus of compelling material. It understands that various audiences have distinct demands and interests. Businesses can generate content that seems personalized and relevant by personalizing messages to certain audience segments. This method not only boosts engagement but also exhibits a knowledge of the audience's individuality.

Creating a Distinctive Voice

A distinct brand voice distinguishes content from the competitors. It's the particular personality and tone that give a content personality. A consistent brand voice, whether it's humor, empathy, or authority, makes content instantly recognized and fosters a sense of familiarity and trust.

The Importance of Empathy

Empathy is a key component of compelling content. It entails putting yourself in the shoes of the audience and gaining a grasp of their problems, desires, and emotions. Empathetic content shows that the brand actually cares about the audience's well-being and wants to deliver value that goes beyond just promotion.

Techniques for Telling Stories
Storytelling is an effective strategy for creating engaging material. It entails organizing content in the form of a narrative, replete with characters, conflict, and resolution. Storytelling engages the audience, keeps them invested, and creates a lasting impact, whether it's a customer success story, a behind-the-scenes look, or a brand origin story.

The Content Formats That Work
Engaging material is available in a variety of formats to accommodate a wide range of preferences and consumption habits. The following formats are popular with audiences:

•**Long-form:** Content such as blog posts and articles that provide in-depth insights, tips, or analyses.

Videos are visual pieces of content that can convey information, elicit emotions, or tell a story.

•Infographics: Simple visual representations of complicated information or data.

Social media posts are short and intriguing content snippets that pique people's interest and encourage conversation.

•Podcasts: Audio content that provides useful information, interviews, or storytelling.

•Measuring Participation and Impact
Various criteria can be used to assess the success of compelling content, including:

Likes, shares, comments, and click-through rates show the level of audience participation and interest.

•Conversion Rates: The percentage of users who take a desired action after engaging with content, such as signing up for a newsletter or purchasing.

•Time Spent: How long people spend viewing material reveals their level of involvement and interest.

CHAPTER 5

LEVERAGING SOCIAL MEDIA: MAXIMIZING ONLINE IMPACT

Social media has become a vital part of our lives in the digital age, affecting the way we connect, communicate, and consume information. The fifth chapter, "Leveraging Social Media: Maximizing Online Impact," digs into the fascinating world of social media marketing, examining how organizations can use it to connect with consumers, develop brand awareness, and drive meaningful interaction. Businesses who grasp the art of exploiting social media can uncover a world of opportunity and catapult their online presence to new heights.

The Revolution in Social Media

The development of social media has brought about a fundamental shift in how businesses connect with their customers. Platforms such as Facebook, Instagram, Twitter, LinkedIn, and TikTok have evolved into virtual town squares where people can openly exchange opinions, trends, and ideas. This chapter emphasizes the importance of using social media as a dynamic medium for true communication and relationship-building rather than just a marketing tool.

The Influence of Connection

Social media is really about human interaction. It's a place where businesses can communicate directly with their customers, listen to their criticism, and respond in real time. Genuine discussions generate a sense of community and trust, transforming casual followers into loyal advocates who feel seen, heard, and respected.

Platforms and Target Audiences

Using social media effectively begins with a thorough understanding of the platforms and their respective audiences. Platforms cater to a wide range of demographics, interests, and communication styles. Businesses may maximize their reach and impact by picking the correct platforms that correspond with their target demographic.

•**Facebook:** A diverse platform with a large user base that is suited for a wide range of industries and content types.

•**Instagram:** A visual platform ideal for presenting products, lifestyle content, and behind-the-scenes peeks.

•**Twitter:** Short and to-the-point, Twitter is great for real-time updates, news, and engaging with popular subjects.

•**LinkedIn:** For professional and business-related contacts, thought leadership, and networking.

•TikTok: Short-form video content aimed at a younger, trend-conscious audience.

Creating Interesting Content

Content that resonates with the audience is essential for effective social media marketing. Engaging content grabs people's attention, starts conversations, and encourages sharing. Here are some ideas for developing compelling social media content:

•Visual Appeal: Make use of high-quality photographs, videos, and graphics that are consistent with your brand's identity.

•Storytelling: Tell stories that elicit emotions, highlight consumer experiences, or illustrate the path of your business.

•User-Generated material (UGC): Encourage customers to share their own material that features your products or services.

•Hashtags: Use relevant hashtags to boost visibility and participate in industry-related conversations.

•Polls and Surveys: Involve your audience by soliciting their feedback and choices.

Behind-the-Scenes: Showcase your staff, office, or manufacturing process to humanize your business.

Educational Content: Provide useful information, suggestions, or lessons that are relevant to your target audience's interests.

Participation and Interaction

It is more than just putting material on social media; it is about developing meaningful conversations. Responding to comments, mentioning people, and participating in dialogues foster a sense of connection and genuineness. Social media is a two-way street; actively listening to and addressing your audience's thoughts and issues creates trust and loyalty.

Partnerships with Influencers

Collaborating with social media influencers might help you make a bigger impact online. Influencers have developed credibility and a loyal following, making them great brand advocates. By collaborating with influencers, you may gain access to their audience and leverage their knowledge to reach new potential clients.

Paid Promotion
Businesses can target certain demographics, interests, and behaviors using social media platforms' sophisticated advertising possibilities. Paid advertising can increase brand awareness, drive website traffic, and aid in lead creation. Businesses may maximize their return on investment and increase their online influence by allocating advertising dollars intelligently.

Insights and analytics
Measuring the success of social media operations is critical for optimizing strategy and outcomes. Social media networks offer analytics and insights that provide useful information about interaction, reach, and audience demographics. Analyzing these indicators assists firms in understanding what works, identifying areas for improvement, and making data-driven decisions.

Strategy and Consistency

In social media marketing, consistency is essential. Maintaining a consistent publishing schedule and a similar brand voice across platforms develops familiarity and helps to build a strong online presence. A well-defined social media strategy specifies objectives, target audiences, content themes, posting frequency, and engagement strategies.

Overcoming Obstacles

While social media has many benefits, it also has drawbacks such as unpleasant comments, disinformation, and algorithm adjustments. To retain brand reputation, businesses must be prepared to tackle these difficulties with transparency, empathy, and a proactive approach.

CHAPTER 6

EXTENDING BEYOND SCREENS: TAKING MARKETING OFFLINE

Taking marketing offline may seem contradictory in an increasingly digital environment. Chapter 6, "Extending Beyond Screens: Taking Marketing Offline," on the other hand, delves into the strong ideas and approaches that enable firms to interact with their audience in actual, real-world ways. Businesses can create memorable experiences, form enduring relationships, and forge a deeper connection that transcends pixels and screens by expanding beyond the virtual domain and engaging customers offline.

Researching the Tangible
There is an inherent draw to tangible experiences in the age of screens and digital interfaces. Offline marketing

capitalizes on this desire for tactile contact, providing a welcome respite from the digital chaos. It includes a wide range of approaches, from in-person events and experience marketing to print materials and physical touchpoints, all of which are intended to engage the senses and create an impression

The Influence of Face-to-Face Communication
Face-to-face encounters have a certain power that cannot be matched online. Human contact, whether it's a handshake, a smile, or a genuine discussion, creates authenticity and generates trust. Offline marketing takes use of these connections, allowing firms to connect with customers on a more personal level, understand their needs, and create memorable moments that last long after the interaction.

Organizing In-Person Events
Offline marketing relies heavily on in-person events. Events give a platform for businesses to exhibit their services, interact with customers, and create an immersive brand experience, whether it's a product launch, a workshop, a trade fair, or a community meeting. Events that are well-executed have the ability to generate awareness, foster brand loyalty, and leave participants with a favorable impression.

Exploratory Marketing

Experiential marketing elevates customer engagement by immersing them in multidimensional encounters. It's about producing memorable moments that have emotional and intellectual resonance. Experiential marketing, which includes everything from pop-up stores and interactive exhibits to live demonstrations and hands-on activities, enables customers to actively participate, forming bonds that go beyond transactional transactions.

Print and direct mail collateral

While digital communication is prevalent, the tactile texture of print materials has its own distinct attraction. Direct mail, brochures, catalogs, and flyers provide a physical touchpoint that draws attention and engages the senses. The act of holding print collateral can create a sense of importance and value, making the brand message more memorable.

Insurgent Marketing

Guerrilla marketing focuses on surprise and innovation, frequently utilizing unexpected approaches to catch people off guard and leave a lasting impression. It entails thinking outside the box and coming up with novel ways to engage the audience in unexpected places and occasions. Guerrilla marketing initiatives are meant to start dialogues and generate buzz, and they frequently rely on social sharing to do so.

Community Development

Offline marketing allows you to develop a sense of community among your customers. Businesses can offer locations for like-minded individuals to connect, exchange experiences, and establish ties through local events, meetups, and workshops. Community-building activities increase brand loyalty, promote word-of-mouth marketing, and foster a sense of belonging.

Increased Online and Offline Synergy

Offline and online marketing are not mutually incompatible; they can complement each other to increase their impact. An in-person event, for example, can be marketed via social media channels, raising excitement and motivating attendees to share their experiences online. Similarly, with targeted promotions and incentives, online advertising can increase offline foot traffic.

Determining Offline Impact

Measuring the impact of offline marketing initiatives can be difficult because they frequently entail less quantitative variables than online analytics. Businesses, on the other hand, can use a variety of ways to assess effectiveness, such as:

•**Attendee Engagement**: During in-person events, assess attendee engagement, feedback, and participation levels.

•**Brand Recall**: Measuring how effectively people recall and associate the brand following offline interactions.

•**Social Media Mentions**: Monitoring online discussions and social media mentions of offline events or experiences.

•**Customer Surveys:** Collecting comments and insights from customers who have participated in offline marketing campaigns.

•**How to Balance Resources and Strategies**

While offline marketing has different advantages, it is critical to combine offline and online techniques based on the target demographic, corporate goals, and available resources. A thorough and effective marketing plan is ensured by a holistic approach that integrates both spheres.

CHAPTER 7

MEASURING PROGRESS: TRACKING AND IMPROVING RESULTS

The ability to evaluate progress and track achievements is not only a beneficial talent in the ever-changing landscape of marketing; it is a fundamental necessity. "Measuring Progress: Tracking and Improving Results," Chapter 7, examines the crucial role of data-driven insights and analytics in leading effective marketing strategies. Businesses may acquire a deeper knowledge of their efforts, make informed decisions, and continuously improve their marketing outcomes by leveraging the power of measurement.

The Value of Measurement

At its foundation, marketing measurement is about gaining insights that inform strategic decisions, not merely numbers and measurements. Measurement gives the insight needed to improve efforts and achieve significant results, whether it's measuring the efficacy of a campaign, tracking consumer behavior, or calculating ROI. Businesses risk operating in the dark without adequate measurement, making decisions based on assumptions rather than evidence.

Setting Specific Goals

Setting clear and detailed objectives is the first step toward effective measurement. What is the intended result of a marketing campaign? Do you want to raise brand exposure, enhance revenue, or improve consumer engagement? Businesses provide a benchmark against which progress may be measured by defining measurable goals.

KPIs (Key Performance Indicators)

Key Performance Indicators (KPIs) are measures used to assess the success of a marketing campaign. They provide a measurable approach to track progress and determine whether goals are being accomplished. KPIs vary based on the campaign's aims and strategy, but popular examples include:

•**Conversion Rate**: The percentage of users who complete a desired action, such as making a purchase or subscribing to a newsletter.

The percentage of persons who click on a link or call-to-action within a marketing message (CTR).

•**Customer Acquisition Cost** (CAC): The price of acquiring a new customer.

•**Return on Investment** (ROI): The ratio of net return to marketing investment cost.

Likes, shares, comments, and social media engagements that demonstrate audience involvement are examples of engagement metrics.

Data Gathering and Analysis

Accurate measurement is dependent on thorough data gathering and processing. Data is collected by businesses from a variety of sources, including website analytics, social media platforms, email marketing software, and customer relationship management (CRM) systems. This data analysis reveals trends, patterns, and insights that provide a holistic picture of the performance of marketing campaigns.

The Impact of Technology

Technology is critical in measuring in the digital age. Marketing automation tools, data analytics platforms, and customer tracking software give firms the tools they need to successfully collect, organize, and analyze data.

These tools simplify measurement and allow firms to make data-driven decisions in real time.

Experimentation and A/B testing

A/B testing, often known as split testing, compares two versions of a marketing feature to see which works better. Businesses can uncover methods that resonate most with their audience by testing variables such as email subject lines, ad language, and website design. Experimentation promotes constant marketing approach improvement and refinement.

Adaptation and Optimization

Measurement is a continuous process of adaptation and optimization, not a one-time event. Businesses employ data analysis insights to make educated changes to their marketing strategies. This could include reallocating money, improving messaging, or experimenting with new media. Effective marketing requires the capacity to pivot based on data-driven insights.

The Human Factor

While data and analytics are strong tools in their own right, they are most effective when supplemented with human interpretation and knowledge. Skilled marketers can extract valuable insights from data and turn numbers into practical strategies. Businesses may make informed decisions based on data-driven insights and human intuition.

Continuous Improvement and Learning

Measuring and improving are inextricably related. Businesses that place an emphasis on measuring foster a culture of continual learning and growth. Businesses ensure that their marketing efforts remain relevant, successful, and aligned with growing client preferences by periodically analyzing results and identifying areas for growth.

Overcoming Obstacles

While measurement has many advantages, firms must deal with issues such as data privacy, data accuracy, and the complexities of interpreting metrics. Businesses may mitigate these hurdles and derive useful insights from their measurement efforts by remaining informed about industry best practices, investing in trustworthy data collection methods, and obtaining advice from experts.

CHAPTER 8

LEARNING FROM SUCCESS: GAINING INSIGHTS FROM ACHIEVEMENTS

In the marketing journey, success is more than just a destination; it is a significant source of knowledge that can illuminate the way forward. "Learning from Success: Gaining Insights from Achievements," Chapter 8, dives into the process of examining and using successful marketing ventures in order to gain vital lessons and develop strategy. Businesses may find patterns, establish best practices, and build an innovative culture that propels them to long-term success by researching their achievements.

The Influence of Reflection

Marketing success is an accomplishment to be celebrated, but it is also a time for reflection and analysis. Businesses can obtain a better knowledge of what works and why by studying the variables that contributed to their success. Reflecting on accomplishments provides a lens through which firms can see their strengths, flaws, and areas for development

Rebuilding Success

Learning from success entails disassembling the elements that resulted in beneficial outcomes. This procedure entails the following steps:

Identifying Key Factors: Identify the precise strategies, methods, and decisions that contributed to success. Was it a strategic alliance, a well-timed social media campaign, or an engaging storytelling approach?

Audience Response Analysis: Examine how the target audience reacted to the marketing activity. What struck a chord with them? Did the content elicit a specific emotion? Understanding audience reactions can help you communicate more effectively.

Measuring Impact: Calculate the impact of a successful campaign using indicators like engagement rates, conversion rates, and revenue growth. Determine how the campaign affected company objectives.

Considering Timing and Context: Consider the timing and context of the effective marketing activity. What current events, trends, or seasonal variables had a role in the success?

Assessing Collaboration: Recognize the importance of teamwork and collaboration in attaining success. Were there any internal or external partners who made a significant contribution?

Importing Best Practices

Marketing activities that are successful frequently disclose best practices that can be applied to future endeavors. Businesses construct a playbook of techniques that have proven to be productive by extracting these practices. Among these practices are:

•**Storytelling Mastery:** Learning how to create captivating narratives that provoke emotional responses from the audience.

•**Audience-Centric** Approach: Prioritizing the target audience's needs, preferences, and behaviors in all marketing initiatives.

•**Seamless Integration:** Developing a unified and integrated marketing strategy that uses many channels to maximum impact.

•**Data-Driven Decision-Making:** Using data and analytics to inform strategies and make educated modifications in real time.

•**Agility and Adaptability:** Adapting to changes in the market landscape, customer behavior, and industry trends.

•**Authenticity and Transparency:** Establishing trust with customers through open and honest communication.

•**Continuous Learning:** Developing a continuous learning, experimentation, and improvement mindset.

Using Insights to Drive Innovation

Insights generated from successful marketing activities inspire new ideas and techniques, which fuels innovation. Businesses can use these insights to develop new campaigns or tactics, adjusting and expanding on what has already proven effective. Businesses maintain their marketing efforts contemporary and forward-thinking by continually looking for ways to push boundaries and explore unexplored territory.

Knowledge Sharing Across Teams

When learning from success, transparency and knowledge-sharing are critical. Marketing insights that are successful should be shared across teams and departments, promoting a culture of collaboration and cross-functional learning. When multiple teams have access to useful information, it promotes collective growth and the implementation of successful strategies to many aspects of the organization.

Adopting a Growth Mindset
Learning from success is not only examining what went right, but also viewing failures and setbacks as opportunities for growth. A growth mindset enables firms to consider obstacles as learning opportunities and to look for ways to develop, innovate, and adapt on a continuous basis.

How to Balance Replication and Innovation
While learning from success entails duplicating effective techniques, it is also critical to strike a balance between replication and invention. Replacing earlier triumphs without taking into account the changing needs of the

audience or the changing market landscape may lead to stagnation. Businesses must strike a balance between employing tried-and-true techniques and seeking fresh growth opportunities

CONCLUSION

EMBRACING SIMPLICITY FOR LASTING IMPACT : THE POWER OF SIMPLE MARKETING

The charm of simplicity shines brighter than ever in a world defined by incessant noise and complication. The path described in this book, "Embracing Simplicity for Lasting Impact: The Power of Simple Marketing," has led us through the complexities of using simplicity as a transforming force in marketing. This final chapter comments on the profound insights obtained, the long-lasting impact of simplicity, and the critical role it plays in determining the future of marketing strategy.

The Essence of Simplicity Revealed

We've looked at the many different aspects of simplicity in marketing in previous chapters. The theme of simplicity has threaded through every aspect, from the core concepts of recognizing audience needs and generating compelling content to embracing offline encounters and learning from accomplishments. It's not just about brevity or minimalism; it's about distilling communications to their essence and making them universally accessible and resonant.

The Resilience of Clear Communication

Clear communication - the ability to transmit messages in a way that is simply understandable and deeply meaningful - is at the foundation of simplicity. The capacity of simple marketing to transcend language borders, cultural differences, and technical complexities demonstrates its potency. Simple messages are not watered down; they are polished, strong, and capable of leaving an indelible impact on the audience's minds and hearts.

Navigating the Digital Terrain

In an era dominated by digital platforms, the influence of minimalism is especially pronounced. Online environments are overflowing with content, and attention spans are short. Simple marketing serves as a beacon, guiding viewers through the digital chaos and capturing their attention with clarity and purpose. Simplicity is the key to engagement and connection, whether it's a succinct email subject line, a minimalist website design, or a clear social media post.

The Power of Tangibility Beyond Screens

While internet interactions are prevalent, the book emphasizes the value of conducting marketing offline. Experiential events, simple design, and tangible connections are examples of ways to extend simplicity beyond screens. The attractiveness of physical experiences and the strength of face-to-face conversations highlight the ageless nature of simplicity in building lasting connections.

A Pathway to Success Through Learning

The chapters on learning from success remind us that simplicity can be a powerful teacher. Businesses can learn significant lessons by deconstructing achievements, finding best practices, and cultivating an innovative culture. The ability to distill success into actionable insights enables firms to capitalize on their strengths, make educated decisions, and evolve continuously.

Building the Future: The Importance of Simplicity

As we end our examination of the role of simplicity in marketing, it is critical to realize its continuous significance and promise. Simplicity is not a passing fad; it is a timeless idea that serves as a beacon in an ever-changing marketing landscape. Businesses that embrace simplicity will continue to succeed and leave a lasting effect in a world where information overload is a daily issue.

Embracing the Difficulty: The Journey Continues

Adopting minimalism is not without its difficulties. Pursuing simplicity in a complicated environment necessitates a dedication to clarity, refinement, and constant development. It takes a desire to pare down messages to their essence and to believe in the power of less. The quest for simplicity is continual, and the benefits are limitless.

The Future: A Long-Term Impact

As we come to the end of this chapter on "Embracing Simplicity for Lasting Impact: The Power of Simple Marketing," it's evident that simplicity is more than just a marketing strategy; it's a philosophy that governs how we communicate, interact, and connect. Simple marketing has the ability to transcend trends and fads, striking a deep chord with people across time and geography. As businesses negotiate the ever-changing marketing landscape, they do so with the understanding that simplicity has the eternal capacity to produce a lasting impact that transcends boundaries, generating an impression that lingers in the minds of customers and echoes into the annals of company history.